© 1990 Franklin Watts

Franklin Watts Inc.
387 Park Avenue South
New York, N.Y. 10016

Library of Congress Cataloging-in-Publication Data
Pluckrose, Henry Arthur.
    Build it! / Henry Pluckrose.
       p.   cm. — (Ways to)
    Summary: Introduces the many words associated with building and construction.
    ISBN 0-531-14062-8
    1. Building—Juvenile literature.   [1. Building.   2. Vocabulary.]
    I. Title.   II. Series: Pluckrose, Henry Arthur.   Ways to.
    TH149.P57   1990
    690'.014—dc20
                                                      89-49398
                                                         CIP
                                                          AC

Editor: Kate Petty
Design: K & Co

Artwork: Aziz Khan

Printed in Italy by
G. Canale S.p.A., Turin

Ways to....

BUILD *it!*

Henry Pluckrose

Photography by Chris Fairclough

FRANKLIN WATTS

New York • London • Sydney • Toronto

Lots of different materials are used for building.

Many things are built with bricks. Bricks are made from clay and baked to make them hard.

Bricks are joined together with mortar. Mortar is a mixture of sand, cement and water.

Stone is also used for building. It can be sawed into building blocks and shaped with a chisel.

Glass is also a building material. It is usually clear so that it lets the light come through.

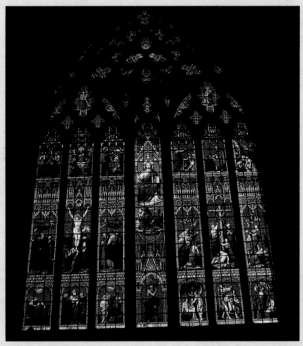

Some things are built in wood. What else is needed for building with wood?

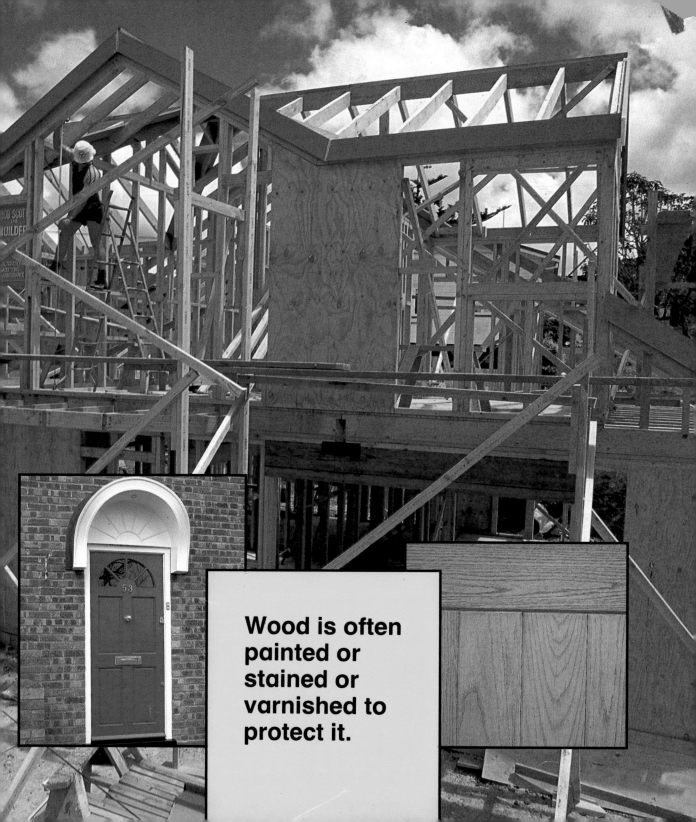

Wood is often painted or stained or varnished to protect it.

Houses can be built from bricks, stone, glass, and wood. What else might be needed...

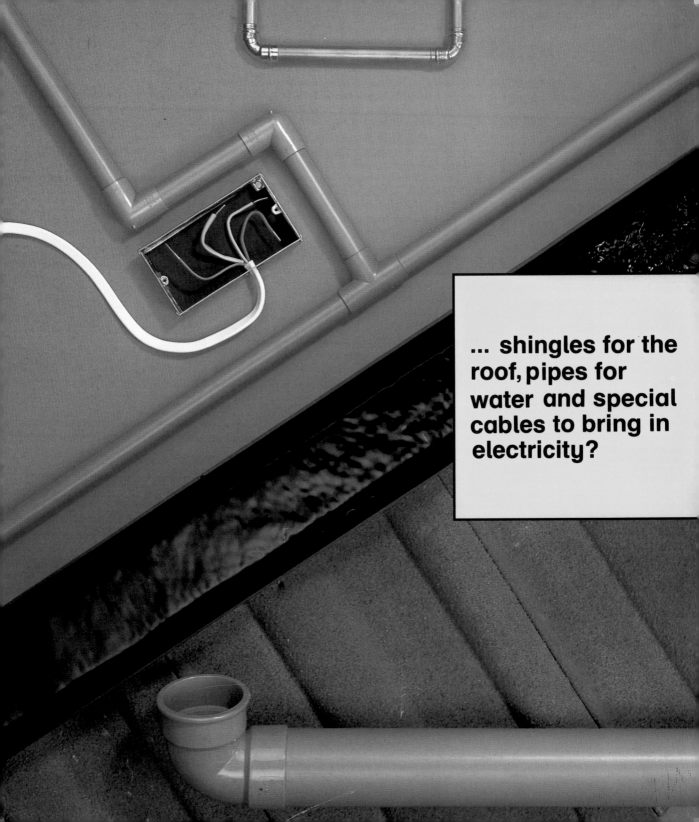

... shingles for the roof, pipes for water and special cables to bring in electricity?

A completed building still needs some finishing touches. Where might you find these?

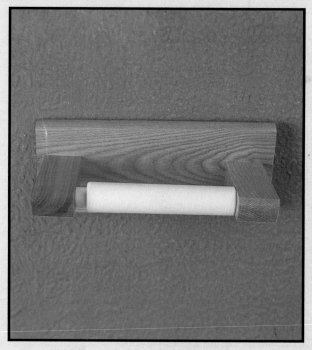

shavers only

200 – 250 v. a c

fused

Buildings give protection from wind and rain, sun and snow. They have to be strong ...

... but even the strongest building may be damaged by storms, floods or earthquakes.

**Homes are built
in different ways
all over the world.**

Sometimes people make homes from the materials that are easiest to get hold of.

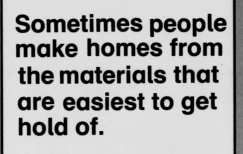

We need buildings for many purposes. Can you match these pictures?

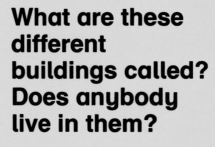

What are these different buildings called? Does anybody live in them?

Things to do

● You can build your own house, palace, castle or town in the sand. First, collect some different shaped containers (yogurt cups, small boxes, toy bucket). Make the sand damp. Pack the containers with damp sand and use them as molds to make your building.

● Use wooden bricks to build a tower. Can you build a tower 8 bricks high? What is the highest tower you can build? Now try to build a tower on a sloping surface. What happens when you try to build high?

● Look at the patterns that bricks make in a wall. Try to find different patterns: some like this

some like this

How many more kinds of pattern can you find?

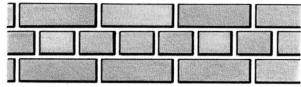

● Find some wooden bricks like these.

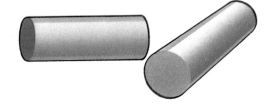

Use them to hold a roof like this.

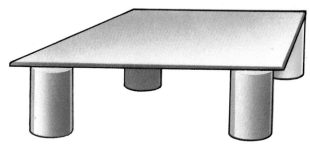

Can you use bricks like these to build a wall?

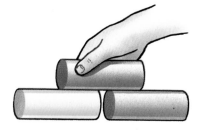

● How many different kinds of things (wood, brick, stone, metal, plastic) have been used to build your school? How many can you find
— on the inside?
— on the outside?

Words about building

	Building materials
add	brick
assemble	cement
builder	concrete
built over	earth
built up	iron
carve	mortar
color	plank
construct	plastic
cover	sand
cut	shingle
decorate	slate
erect	steel
heap	stone
join	tile
make	timber
mass	thatch
paint	wire
pile	wood
produce	
put together	
raise	
shape	
tool